The L Word

a collection of poems

Sherin Francis

BookLeaf Publishing

India | USA | UK

Made with ❤ on the BookLeaf Publishing Platform
www.bookleafpub.in
www.bookleafpub.com

Dedication

for the sea to my sky

Preface

This journey began impulsively, on a long commute from the airport after the best summer of my life. In my deeply sleep-deprived and depleting mental stability that was hanging by a thread, my emotions that twisted in my chest and choked in my throat were captivated by this opportunity for a release.

Whilst poetry has always been deeply personal to me for I can never separate it from my self, I have written most of these more for me than for a reader. Nevertheless, if my musings of anguish, love and identity ring bells even in a faint chime, I am grateful and hope it comforts you in the thought that you are not alone. Experiences may differ but emotions are so rarely original; allow yourself the solace that what connects us runs deeper than the surface, it always has.

When you feel that the world is crashing down upon you, please look up at the sky. For even after the darkest night, the sun always rises. Happiness may not be permanent, but remember neither is sadness.

No matter what, the sun will rise. We just need to wait.

Acknowledgements

I cannot possibly begin this without thanking my precious sister, for buying me LaBrioche and never batting an eye at me while I was almost near tears from the anxiety. You don't even remember it but it was a core memory for me, one that I am eternally grateful for. You built a circle on the day I was born as you held my small hand tightly and vowed to protect me forever—be it against stupid bullying boys to life's daily hindrances. In any and every minor inconvenience in my life, you are my go-to, my 911. Thank you for your services throughout my life, please keep me subscribed till the end.

This would be incomplete without my ultimate support system and hype-duo, Clint and Cliffy. You've been pillars of strength and solidarity literally for all my life, but especially when I needed it the most. There are not enough words in any language on Earth (and definitely not enough pages) to suffice all the gratitude and love that I have towards you both. Having the circle that's always got your back and is a safety net is **so** important and I'm so glad you two have weaved one strong enough to withstand age, distance and time.

Thank you to Lee, a constant from our most troubling teen to our even more troubling twenties. We haven't spoken in ages but there's not a yellow vehicle that crosses by where I don't immediately miss you. You've always called me your saviour from back when we're in school but you've saved me from my own demons just as much. Even though we're working on saving ourselves now and having bi-yearly catch-ups, I will always be grateful for you for while my heart knows distance, my love does not.

Surprise entry will be to my mother. You may never read this but thank you. It killed me to write no.7 but I am so unbelievably grateful for the kindness and patience you have shown me, for immediately reassuring me that you could never hate me. When carried for as long as they have been, secrets begin to whisper and when you hear them for long enough, you start to believe them. You wiped them all away with that single hug by the door, by holding my hand and telling me you still love me. I love you, Omma.

Honorable mention to the Lesbian Renaissance Movement of 2024—Chappell Roan, Renee Rapp, Billie Eilish, King Princess, Hayley Kiyoko, girl in red, Fletcher, Clairo, Phoebe Ryan, dodie, boygenius, Lana del Rey and of course, Hozier. You have been the repeat soundtrack for this entire work and god, it's been fantastic.

And finally, to my pink skies, to the sea to my sky. My love, my other half, my wife. You've read almost all of these but I hope that it doesn't take away from knowing that it's you, it's you, this is all for you. The only heaven I'll be sent to is truly a place on Earth with you.

Our hearts know distance but our love will not. And it never will. I love you, my darling.

1. of longing

I met you when I was seventeen and I never knew
the road that lay ahead of us, how they would
interweave
if we were to tell either of our past selves, neither would
believe
starcrossed as it is, no part of it would ever ring true

it took us a couple years to finally start talking
I can't pinpoint when exactly I began falling
all I recall vividly is the pounding of my heart
as I willed it to slow down, for my feelings to stay apart
imagine being a cliché, falling for the straight best friend
could anything even start when it was already doomed
to end

between pages and lyrics shared, I'd breathe you in
choking on your smile as my heart twisted within
distancing and doing everything I could to pull away
with every message you sent, I couldn't help but stay
a single glance my way and like a sandcastle, I crumbled
firmly I once stood, but my disobedient heart fumbled
pretending I didn't have all those fantasies and dreams
you're just another friend, I told myself while my soul
screams

recognising its other half in you was going to be the end
of me

you who is an existence
that drives me to the brink of insanity
keep laughing with me like that
while I succumb to the gravity
falling into an abyss that hurts me
where happiness isn't even a probability
echoing in my head like a haunting melody
I'm bleeding inside, in search for a remedy

years later, I write this now with a profound endearment
for my pining younger self, she was so perseverant
cowardly or resilient, I do not know
but heart-first into the abyss, she did go
and I know we're both better off for it
imagine if I had moved on, if my heart had quit
if I knew then that you've always been my worst habit
an addiction I'd never overcome, that I'd fully commit
to every inch of me, my heart, my life, my soul, I admit
for all I know now is that even as we are miles apart,
this longing has only intensified within my heart
I've longed for you longer than I have had you
my best habit, now after a summer with you, I know it's
true

the best part of me, even when in my arms, I still long
for you

2. of luck

never been one who believed in fate
not since I realised I cannot think straight
never been one to believe in the universe
not when the world has always shown me its true
colours

never been much of a believer at all
far too often felt as if I was praying to a wall
coddled, conditioned and conformed to blind belief
a childhood and adolescence that ended in defeat
surrendering to the harrowing reality of the unknown
the alienation of the realisation that we are all alone

yet these days I find myself wondering
of all the roads I did not take, the ones far more travelled
from my passion for the arts, a war I had long battled
to the very place that brought me to you
a fleeting impulsive decision for us two
from that very first day when I noticed you
to our missed opportunity in the library too

I think of how literature saved me as a child
in an unstable house and with a disturbed mind
how it lit a fire that would burn and blaze to this day

how in a world of black and white, it would be my grey
I think of how the sight and smell of blood makes you
faint
how if it weren't for that, our first chapter would be
replaced
how it could have taken you down a different road
one where I wouldn't have been, where we'd be alone

I think of your father in my hometown
before either of us were even around
I wonder if our fathers crossed paths with each other
if a star winked in the sky then, foreseeing the lover
the two that, in a different city, would find one another
oblivious themselves of the love that lay ahead
precious like stardust that the desert skies bled

never been one to believe in fate
never thought I was one to wait
never been much of a believer
look how far we've come, my dear

3. of lesbians

fourteen years together in a building full of girls
the church at our entrance, as everyone took turns
talking about the boys across the school, "he's so cute!"
I remember thinking, "who cares about him, I'm looking
at you?"

with their flowy hair, loose tendrils that'd curl on their
neck
their soft hands and long fingers, nails all painted and
perfect
the round cheeks that lift, the laughs to their toothy
smiles
why a girl was often an artist's muse, is easy to realise

before I even realised that I was alone in these thoughts
of admiration, before the heart even knew what it wants
the word was thrown around with a malice that was
palpable
not to be associated with, as I quickly learnt to 'act
natural'
"He's so cute!" nodding eagerly, I found myself saying,
surely, this is temporary, I found myself praying
with a guilt that grew, my visits to the shrine did too

a conscience that felt tainted in a body that felt
desecrated
it wasn't until years later that I could let go of that
hatred

with that release, came the sweet bliss of relief
eyes wide as I soaked in girls in all their entirety—
curves and dips and smooth skin that gleamed,
hair that'd stick to glossy lips as they beamed,
how could anyone look at all those boys across
when goddesses walked amongst us, cue the applause
it wasn't until recently that I'd even let myself be free
encompassed in a word was a liberty I hadn't expected to
feel
the weight of which only bore down on me while my
thighs squeezed your head
never did I think I'd re-realise my sexuality while
writhing in your bed
lesbianism, I found myself thanking that abandoned
shrine from then
feeling blessed to not wait to get hard, as I moaned for
you to do it again

4. of lipstick

an experiment with self-love that I began at seventeen
is now a collection of colours and brands, my identity
the smile it brings me when someone doesn't know my
name
but they know me as the girl with lips that never look
the same
in shades of red, wine, pinks, purples and shine
with a mouth this pouty, how can I not cross the line
wearing every colour, wondering which will cross your
mind

imagine my surprise when you tell me you remember
every colour I wore to college, down to the specific shade
while there I was, pining for you every day as I'd wonder
why did you have to be straight, as my heart swayed
and there you were, beautiful eyes that I'd tried to hold
in contact; yet back then, you weren't so bold
but here you are, telling me of rust orange and wine red
colours you'd memorised, while I'd wondered if it was all
in my head
if only I knew that you'd been bold to sneak glances at
me
enough to commit every shade of my lips to your
memory

5. of language

a memory that haunts me to this day
every time that I speak in front of anyone,
is when I was ten and a teacher liked the way
that I read aloud in class and lo, there begun
me stumbling over my words and sentences
a praise that should have been encouraging
yet all I could hear was myself fumbling
perhaps that was which prompted me to the pen
for the written word would never fail me, time and time
again

perhaps it is that I was too shy in my earlier years
to even attempt a tongue that was not my mother's
the irony amuses everyone that I have now mastered
the coloniser's vernacular, as my own scattered
struggling to roll my tongue in the way all the others do,
pretending others' taunts don't get to me the way they
do
even though every teasing laugh and remark pierces
through

for I am trying my best, and I wish to be better
in this white land, now, more than ever
I wish to hold on to my 'foreign' tongue

and learn it as I should have when young
if nothing, to understand the songs you hold so dear
that you pin to me and our love, those you're thrilled to
hear
for I know better than anyone, how beauty tends to get
lost in translation, regardless of attempts earnest
for some words capture a moment so finite
even the masters struggle to explain, try as they might

in the years to come, my love, hold onto your patience,
something undeniably romantic in your teaching, so
gracious
is the way you look at me as I spell your name over and
over
how fitting that the first word I learnt to write was that
of my lover

6. of loss

this world that is considered
as a big round globe
when actually it is only a robe
beneath, a glorified graveyard
to a boundless archive of souls
that lay buried underneath
this ground that you walk on
of this big round glove

I think of myself as fortunate enough
to not really know loss in the way others do
seeing others who have had it real tough
makes me grateful to still have all of you

but every time I hear someone call another 'sweetie'
I think of her—taken far too young, far too easy
my first companion in a strange and scary place
I wish I knew her parents, could've given them an
embrace
could've told them even if everyone else forgot, I still
remember her face

but every time I walk past a diner
earlier this evening, past the laughs of a family of four

it serves as yet another cruel reminder
of a childhood that left me at the door
everyone's moved on, am I the only outsider?

but every time I cross before the cemetery
I think of that day in early November
visiting the hyacinths, roses and peonies
freshly cut jasmines, lilies and daisies
all atop the tomb, they lay
adorning the polished stone,
beneath, the bodies still wither away

but every time I find my old books and diaries
there is an ache in my chest, a wound reopening in my
soul
for the girl with her head in the clouds, hands full of
stories
how do I tell her that I have lost my way and lost
control?
a plot that got away from me, this was never the end
goal
it has been such a long time since I truly felt whole

in this big round globe
are there many more
walking graveyards
or am I the only empty soul?

7. of lies

what's in a name, what's in a lie
if it's unknown to you, does it matter why
I felt the need to hide, am I not justified?

"some things are better left unsaid"
a saying that you had drilled into my head
from when I was a kid, you taught me a white lie
you wouldn't call it that, but you didn't have to try
from when I was young, I had much to hide
somewhere between what was white and not alright
the lines between the lies became a blurry sight
as I fumbled between the lines of what was right
you asked me why I didn't say anything that night
don't you know I've always been quicker to flight
parenting myself in a house that got loud some nights
I learnt to be quiet, knowing what it meant if I did fight

what's in a name, what's in a lie
don't you see it made me too want to die?
this was not a secret I wished to keep from you
this was a secret with a weight I did not know to hold
so please don't look at me with those eyes
as if I knowingly committed this crime
it took me all my childhood and adolescence to realise

that what I held within my hands was not a knife
not a weapon meant to hurt you nor I
just a misunderstood love I couldn't deny

I'm incredibly tired of living in this lie
it's not really as terrible as you fear
I'm so tired of wishing I would die
I know you worry they will all sneer
but I'd rather take that on than continue to deny
what makes me feel like me, my dear

my name is the same, there is no lie,
not in who I am, who you knew me to be
tell me that you are not ashamed
that you still love me just the same

8. of lumière

you wield so much more power than you know
a single message from you is enough to calm my soul
if only you knew the extent of the power you have over
me
cause darling, you see the very best version of me

twenty-five years that have been spent looking over
always counting down, another month, another year
why, god, did it take me so fucking long to discover
that after all this time, the grass is always going to be
greener
I've been running for so long, I don't even know what
I'm after

the new year and summer that I spent in your arms
feeling lighter than air, the most present I've ever been
to feel safe and sound, a head without any alarms
the realisation that you are my life's greatest win
the light with which you hold me,
the light in your eyes when you look at me,
the light you lit within my chest that set me free
from this darkness of the void that had me at sea
drowning for years, with my arms flailing desperately
until your hand finally reached out and found me

I may be the sky, sunny and then stormy
unpredictable, I bring you in all its glory
but as my rippling sea, you always meet me
on the horizon, where the sun sets us free
for when the rays fall upon us, it is gorgeous
golden hour has never looked so divine until it was on
us

9. of lust

if I close my eyes and press my fingers to my lips
I can still taste the lips between your hips
still see that look you got in your eyes
while my head was between your thighs
our parted lips meeting, too breathless to kiss
how even the air around us crackled with bliss

the distance always makes it harder
but on many occasions, I did wonder
if it was the dreams and months of longing
that made us so feral at what we were doing
being so insanely good even for a first time
had me gripping the sheets and chanting in rhyme
feeling a delirium that can only be deemed a crime
how I'd crumble and fall apart at your slightest touch
how my mouth couldn't stop until your skin was flush

if I close my eyes and recall that night
I don't even have to try too hard, an ever-present sight
the memory of you squirming away from me,
from my relentless fingers, my greedy tongue
your back sprawled right beneath me
a memory that I frequent—against me, you lay undone

the way you'd pinned me against your wall,
pressing your body to me like I was all you'd ever need
my hands gripping your thigh, bunching up your dress
your mouth on a solo mission to turn my makeup into a
mess
every breath, touch and kiss—you love to make me moan
sounds that are new to even my ears—all yours to own
how we stayed upright that day, I'll never know
you were making me fall all over again, fast and then
slow

if I close my eyes I can still hear
the music we played, all so clear
that sinfully delicious playlist we can't listen to anymore
they don't hit quite the same as they did all those times
not without your moans as you shook to your core
to harmonise like a backing track, watching your chest
rise
holding you as you caught your breath, feasting with my
eyes
as your eyes flickered, your hand reaching for mine
for even in blissful delirium, you hold onto me
there is no spirit on earth that could take you away from
me
god save their souls if they ever dare to
our kind of fire, the desire I hold for you
heaven is not fit for a love like you and I

it's the kind of love that'd bring down the sky
one that knows no bounds, being separated as long as we
are
perhaps the devil knew the lust burning in us could
make the earth shatter
the two of us together, a force to be reckoned with, a
pleasure like no other

10. of laughter

favourite laugh number five has to be
the one where we forgot momentarily
privy to an audience, yet you did speak
at the table, revealing what I do in my sleep
at his comment, you buried your head almost shyly
while I looked like a maniac, just grinning widely

favourite laugh number four has to be
the muffled one in the dark, almost secretly
as you tried to squirm away from me,
the water spilling across your skin like a treat
that I immediately claimed, not pausing for a beat
you were thirsty but I still needed to eat

favourite laugh number three has to be
your head above mine, looking down at me
the slight jerk and chortle when I bit down stubbornly
the disbelief as your tied your hair back quickly
how dare you take your hands off of me?
your hair can wait, pay attention to me

favourite laugh number two has to be
my personal favourite, the one of incredulity
you know the one, that escaped so breathlessly

as I pulled away, having just feasted like a queen
coming off a high as I sucked my fingers clean
you wanted lunch, I was still wearing your sheen

favourite laugh number one has to be
your favourite, where I was far too keen
fingers merely grazing my hair and I was moaning
all I recall now is the way you wouldn't stop giggling
don't you know all I wanted was for you to touch me
of *course* I'm folding as all yours for the taking, easy

11. of liquor

Whiskey as my starter, the appetiser
 smooth and clean, I fell helplessly
 a wide glass, crystalline and open
 taking swigs, flowing with the motion
 a slow dull of senses as moments passed by
 missed opportunities that you'll never let die

Vodka for my second, the pre-game
 familiarity setting in, changes in name
 flutters that began, secret second glances
 fingers swirling the rim, taking risky chances
 to sneak another look, just one more peek
 I promise I won't fall, I'm not that weak

Tequila as the flutters began to burn
 liquid fire pouring down, I would slowly learn
 my heart was not as steady as my head
 pathetically falling for every word you said
 smiling as I repeat that I love how it hurts
 feelings go away, I don't mind the burns

Brandy as my stomach twists, sick and queasy
 a pain that demanded attention, made me uneasy
 couldn't be ignored any longer, feeling cornered

flutters turned to a numbing ache, replacing the pains
the highs making way for the low, needing you to know
that I couldn't see straight no more, that I'd lost it for
sure

Rum as the mediator, that which transitions
  songs that didn't quite play the same, now all renditions
  coloured—playlists, shows and movies infiltrated by you
  the pretense to be sober, that I never did stop drowning
  not until you realised on that one February evening
  that you weren't alone, that I returned the feelings

Gin as my dessert drink, my clear happy pill
  overdosing on delirious bliss, could I get a refill?
  stealing kisses that taste like alcohol and toothpaste
  don't you think we've had too much time to waste?
  grab your keys and pack all your bags, baby
  don't you want to kiss all this liquor off of me?

12. of lunch

Rome boasts of religion, art and food galore
me, however, I've always been a lesbian whore
while the others admired the Sistine Chapel in awe
it was Michelangelo's glorious sculptures that lured my
eyes
silken-like fabric draped lasciviously over luscious thighs
all the curves and delicate hips carved in such precision
it was crystal why he was a favourite of the religion

you stood across the street, blue across your skin
cinched around your waist, it made my head spin
dress wrapped around you as if an early Christmas
present
to not unwrap you then was a test of patience, utter
torment
was it purposeful, I mused, if you meant to drive me
crazy
vivid recollections of you leaning on me as my sight
went hazy

as if a treasure map, I unstrung everything on you
I, the devoted cartographer, laid you bare to view
while you unfolded, mapped across the sheets;
sunlight bathing your skin, eager eyes reading as I cease

to breathe when my gaze falls upon those sacred stars
speckled across your canvas, singing beneath my palms
like the North Star, guiding my greedy mouth
across the constellations, leading me south
where I found my paradise waiting for me
dripping with gold, it was a treasure to see

her surrounding two pillars gave way impatiently
as if waiting to be discovered, I followed eagerly
for hungry, I was not—I was *starving*
divine glory on my tongue, I was feasting
upon this treasure that I'd dreamed of for ages
heaven could hear the songs of my praises

open, as you lay, fierce still
pillars rising as I have my fill
shutting my ears until I drowned
in gold, as I heard my heart pound
ethereal symphonies leaving your lips
my stubborn fingers digging into the dips
holding my map in place, lest it fly away
X marks the spot, crescent indents to stay
with all the darkening ships across the way
sailed by my lips, placing a memory at bay

13. of lemons

loving you has always been yellow
a colour I'd hated, one that never showed
not in my wardrobe, but since you said that first hello
in Korean, a tinge of it bloomed and flourished
bright streaks across a canvas of monochrome
words do not suffice on how it felt to finally find home

loving you used to be sour
from when we'd text until the late hour
my heart twisting in my chest
my head telling me it'd be for the best
if I stopped while I was ahead
all those sleepless nights in my bed
as if my heart could ever obey
when it spent all night wishing you were gay
but like tequila followed by a lime
it was clockwork every single time
freshly squeezed stings dripping into a gaping wound
pain that became second nature, a love that had me
consumed

loving you finally grew sweet
that February afternoon, a confession finally made
complete

on a weekend, after a cinematic three-day showdown
the words I'd been longing to hear, never sounded so
profound
as if I were a cursed hero, finally been released
blessings abundant—at last, true love is sweet
like warm tea after an exhausting day
light and languid, worth the long wait
slowly swirling spoon, a calm and patient brew
as the leaves change colour, so do you
thought I was the only one falling but you did too

loving you is a citrusy lemon
Sicilian, as if plucked from heaven
smooth yet tangy, like my favourite gin
love that feels this divine, it must be a sin
a love that is not merely the late and risqué Friday night
but the soft bread slathered in lemon curd, toasted just
right
on a late Saturday noon, way past the sunrise
lazy Sunday mornings, as we watch the skies
shift colours around the room, reflected in each other's
eyes
feeling your pulse rise and hearing your morning sighs
—this is all I ever want in life.

14. of leaving

'to Love means to Wait.'
a phrase I think we both secretly hate
mastering the art of patience across these years
as we make it through together, battling all our fears
many still stand tall and proud, not easily knocked down
overpowering at times, as they push our heads until we
drown
on this night where I can feel you struggling to breathe
even as I try to reach out, ready to swim underneath
but you have an awful habit of keeping me at bay
so I lie awake, waiting for night to become day
for that when is you resurface
while I wonder what is my purpose
if not to be the one to hold my love
when she drowns, how can I idly wait above?

on these nights we are left alone to our own devices,
do you wonder too, how much we have left in us?
how much sorrow can we take?
how long will we have to wait?

leaving is as familiar to me as the back of my hand
for as long as I could remember and understand
perhaps my heart has numbed over the years

accustomed to the plane rides, bid adieu to the tears
do not mistake for a moment that this is easier for me
it's a deeply visceral pain, when your heart's out of your
body
across the seas, in a continent farther than where I stand
this is not where I'm meant to be, in this coloniser's land

that day that I left, I left my heart in your room,
close to your chest where I lay my head, I assume
home is not this room that I'm in, not this land where I
stand
—it's in your arms, your embrace, in the palm of your
hand

15. of long distance

I close my eyes every night
picturing your arms around me
the way you'd always hold so tight
even when we had time
as if it was just another dream
as if we would crack and fall apart
fragments that faded, a longing that lingered
countless moments when we would arise
reaching for you instinctively with morning sighs
hands fumbling, desperately tracing over a cold empty
bed
dreams so poignant as if stolen memories running
through my head
still tasting you in phantom embraces
missing your warmth in all these spaces
the ones where you would fit so perfectly
your head below my chin, your forehead against my grin
my neck bearing witness to your muffled laughs
the smile it pulled out of me, feeling as if in a trance
the way my fingers drew feathery circles on your hips
the way I couldn't wait, mouth chasing all your dips
even as you sat up and reached across the bed for water
I was parched myself but all I could speak was desire
with you in my arms, it was a mantra in my head — "all I

need is her"

now I'm back in my cold bed, you in yours
reminiscing over all those days that were ours
that one night in the cool summer as we giggled into
kisses
now I reminiscence, as we miss each other to pieces
waiting and counting down again as we return to cold
reality
dreaming of those days when we can restore our sanity
together, in each other's arms, is where we need to be

16. of loneliness

I find myself lingering in busy streets
the art of noticing, people-watching quietly
a distraction, anything that makes the ache cease
reminding myself it's not so terrible, it's needless anxiety
there's beauty in being lost, in being alone
there's peace in those moments when I come home
the gentle evenings as I stir my cup of tea
quiet laughs that echo in my room emptily
a piece of peace in those calls we have
white noise as we do chores in the back

when the nights are coldest in winter
there's not a single night that goes by
where I don't think, "I wish you were here"
chest aching enough that I feel I might die
it's worse in the rush and chaos of everyday
the distance never gets easier, feeling so far away
the screen goes black, an emptiness that consumes
the void returns, relentless in its pursuit

an advocate for living alone, I have been taunted
by my own past dreams and desires, I am haunted
that which aches me, is not the living alone
what really stings, is the pain of being unknown

a wound that was gashed further during the summer
falling asleep and waking by your side made me discover
the warmth of spooning, skin to skin
my heart to your back, beating within
did you feel it, my love? heartbeats all for you
do you feel it, my love? it aches for you
it misses skipping beneath your touch
the way it would race, all that rush

I picture the apartment, cosy and quaint, years from now
surprising as it may be, I'm still drinking my tea alone
people-watching out my window, the streets below
but the walls have your paintings, many mugs around
décor, throw pillows, a statement wall—colours that
surround
this little space that I no longer call just mine
smiling as you stand beside me with your coffee, our
hands intertwined

17. of lullabies

on those days when I'm in a spiral
drowning far too deep, mind far too idle
I listen to your voice read your writing
you said you love it when I'm reciting
my poetry, my stories, all my feelings I'm confiding

it's bizarre now to think of last September
an abundance of fantasies in my head
every one of which I still vividly remember
didn't know for certain but I still looked ahead
for many nights until that magical December
after those terrible days at work, I'd lay in bed
I'd close my eyes and picture you as I held
onto the last shreds of my sanity, praying to survive
the last of that cold winter, I had a reason to stay alive
to see you again after all these years, it was my only
drive

now I'm back in another cold September
your gift lays waiting for me, it's still wrapped
we have references now instead of merely fantasies
your hands, your lips, I miss wearing your hickeys
back to reminiscing, on all these cold mornings,
recalling your embrace as I listen to your recordings

phantom touches I desperately hold on to, that are
slowly fading
back to lullabies that comfort me, we are back to waiting

18. of Literature

Words and musings—from childhood, have been
 sweet companions amidst misery, whence these fingers
did begin
 to hold a pen while poetry bled and coursed within;

Mightier than the sword, it has always been said
Ne'er did I muse that words become my daily bread
For though they do not feed me nor quench my thirst
A generous lover in dark times witnessing me at my
worst
Gentle and endearing as the futilities of life intercept my
way
Waiting to be penned down, patiently anticipating that
day
For it would never judge, never hold a grudge against me
Unlike others who tolerate inattention far less amicably.

Nay, these musings are glimpses to my soul, a safe haven
Power resting within these fingers that hold creation
For there is nothing
 to learn humankind better—their sorrows, loves and
strife
 than following the ways of a reader, weaving the
threads of life.

19. of legacy

a childhood fostered in the writings of many
worlds of talking trees, dragons, magic and fantasy
long before I dared to begin my own musing
it was far more interesting; all these lives I was living

idolising the likes of Coleridge, Dickinson and Keats
admiring the lives, loves and poetic lyricism of the elites
an envy of the mastery engraved in romantic poetry
to learn of those whose pens inked gold in years of glory
far too brief, most of them taken too early

when I was younger, I would naively wonder
if someone would come across my own words, years
later
would my legacy be poorly written heteronormativity?
penned when too impressionable, when lacking
originality
would they know of my love for all things fantasy?
would they make a timeline of all my depressing poetry?

would anyone discover all those embarrassing diary
entries?
my battles with religion and identity that followed me
into my twenties

would they reckon that I was far too mentally unstable?
or would I strike a chord of familiarity, would I be
relatable?
now in a sea of writers, I do not wonder
instead, I write for me and for my lover
regardless of if I'm discovered, of what remains of me,
I refuse to leave even a sliver of doubt, no one will
disagree
with who you are to me—not a roommate nor close
friend nor enemy

all my handwritten letters, do not mistake the way
for even when pretending to be just a friend, it was in
plain display
read how I worship her, how she is half my soul—I, the
poet, say
how I'd recognise her touch blind, how my heart daren't
sway
it chose her as my purpose, my muse, forever to stay
come months or years, day or night—for her, I will wait

20. of lessons learned

at fifteen, I thought I was old enough
my sister was twenty and she was mature
at fifteen, I was certain I was tough,
I knew what I'd do at twenty, I was sure

at eighteen, I thought I would feel legal
everyone always made such a fuss, the people
at eighteen, I thought I knew where I'd be at twenty
my life lay before me in stages, every phase planned
plenty

at twenty, I found myself wondering if I could go home
if I'd see my parents again, if the world was ending now
I found myself confessing to you, knowing I had nothing
to lose
if we were to die in this lockdown, to let my love die
unknown, I refuse

now at twenty-five, in a world more alienating than I've
ever been
my sister nearing thirty, a new chapter for her and her
children begins
I'm realising that this feeling of just being a kid is always
within

did Peter know that although with growing up, we rarely
get the wins
being a lost boy is something that we all grow around
instead of pushing through it, it's a feeling we push
down
pretending to have it together, to know what we are
doing
is all adulthood really is—to smile and nod even when
you're breaking

the apartment abroad with the fancy skyline that I
chased as a teen
that was once a dream is now something that lies
between
an unattainable fantasy or for a me in an alternate
reality
as now between my dead-end 9-to-5 and my weekends
that disappear
in the blink of an eye, I countdown to my next flight out
of here
the highs that I chase now are in the warmth of the faces
that wait for me
the arms that embrace me, drinking the nights I dance
away blissfully
with all my favourite people surrounding me, no longer
separated by sea
for happiness is fleeting, serotonin and dopamine that

leave me in a stupor

hold on, teenage me, the apartment may not be but you
are happier than you were

21. of love.

she walked into my life like a silent tide
hidden amidst the faces, behind polite smiles
as the moon peeked, she gleamed in the light
gentle ripples as stars burned bright in her eyes
my own, catching her shine across the lines
that stood between us, deep and dark desires
light would hide not for the heart is loud
the truth can only be masked for so long
it must shine through somehow
in handwritten letters, dreams, a hidden vow
that no matter what happened, I'd still be around
occanic waves like home, crashing into each other
meeting me at the horizon, where we belong together
many moons later, the stars finally aligned
giving way to our hearts, as we both dived
into the deep end, hands and mouths meeting
a long awaited kiss, as the sun was finally rising
diamonds speckled, bouncing from my stars to you
rippling pools of glitter, a truly ethereal view
for they say love is patient, love is kind,
a love that took some tries, to bloom it took a while,
you know it's love when it hurts,
when it's both a blessing and a curse
it's love when pink skies make us smile,

when it brings warmth despite all the miles
your existence driving me to the brink of insanity
keep holding me as we succumb to the gravity
basking in our love, a stroke of serendipity
we're floating hand-in-hand, deliriously
blessed be the mystery of love
for you're my other half, gifted from above
made out of stardust, star-crossed are we
precious gold glitter, keep shining for me.

9 789363 302099